PUFFIN BOOKS

CHUCKLE, CHUC
THE CHILDREN'

Why did the angel los
Because of harp failure.

This is a joke book by children for children, for there
are hundreds of jokes of every kind in *Chuckle, Chuckle –
The Children's Joke Book*, all collected from the children
and staff of St Anthony's School, Hampstead, and
selected and arranged by Anne Leadercramer and
Rosalind Morris in aid of the Wishing Well Appeal.
There are 'Doctor, doctor' and 'Waiter, waiter' jokes,
animal jokes, school jokes, cartoons, puzzles, limericks
and crosswords – everything you could ever want from
a joke book and more. Every page is packed with fun to
keep you and your friends chuckling for years, and it's
all in a very good cause as well, for all the royalties from
the book go to support the Wishing Well Appeal to save
Great Ormond Street Children's Hospital.

CHUCKLE, CHUCKLE

THE CHILDREN'S JOKE BOOK

The Children and Staff of
St Anthony's School

*Devised by Anne Leadercramer and
Rosalind Morris*

Introduced by Roald Dahl
Illustrated by Judy Brown

PUFFIN BOOKS

PUFFIN BOOKS

Published by the Penguin Group
27 Wrights Lane, London W8 5TZ, England
Viking Penguin Inc., 40 West 23rd Street, New York, New York 10010, USA
Penguin Books Australia Ltd, Ringwood, Victoria, Australia
Penguin Books Canada Ltd, 2801 John Street, Markham, Ontario, Canada L3R 1B4
Penguin Books (NZ) Ltd, 182–190 Wairau Road, Auckland 10, New Zealand

Penguin Books Ltd, Registered Offices: Harmondsworth, Middlesex, England

First published 1988
10 9 8 7 6 5 4 3 2 1

Filmset in Linotron Baskerville by
Rowland Phototypesetting Ltd,
Bury St Edmunds, Suffolk
Made and printed in Great Britain by
Cox and Wyman Ltd, Reading, Berks

Introduction

I love jokes. Not everyone does. Most people, as they get older, tend to grow out of childish jokes, and the older they get the less funny they find them. Very few really old people are able to raise a smile if you tell them one. But the older I get, the more excruciatingly funny I find them. I suppose, therefore, that I am a sort of infantile geriatric.

Limericks I love best of all. This is perhaps because a really good limerick is such a difficult thing to write. I know hundreds of them by heart, both the simple ones and bawdy ones, and I often recite them to myself when I am alone to cheer me up.

Pomposity is the scourge of old age. Most successful people become progressively more pompous the more ancient and successful they become. They never laugh at childish jokes. They never laugh at anything much. They are miserable creatures.

This little book is a wonderful achievement. It has been made by the children and staff of St Anthony's School in Hampstead and everyone should buy it, not only because many of the jokes in it will make you laugh but also because all the profits are going to the best children's hospital in the world, Great Ormond Street.

Roald Dahl

How the Book Came About

One night when we were having some tea,
We saw Great Ormond Street Hospital on the
    TV.
They said they were going to close it down,
And so we listened with a big frown.

This can't happen, we thought to ourselves.
Now what can we do?
We paced the floor to think some more,
And then the light came shining through.

And so on the next day we issued bags,
To all the teachers,
And all the lads,
All the cooks got them too,
And then we said this is what you must do.

'You can write a poem or tell a joke,
Or anything you like,
And then you will put them
In the bag –
We will give you a fortnight.'

So everybody worked real hard,
As every day went by,
They sat and thought,
And drew and wrote,
Because closing the hospital was no joke.

When the time was over,
St Anthony's was very proud.
They all had worked together,
As one big happy crowd.

'We can make a book of all the things,
And then it can be sold.
And all the money that we get can go to
The hospital so great and bold.'

There was an old lady from Dorset,
Who got in a fix with her corset.
Her plight was so tight,
She died in the night,
That unfortunate old lady from Dorset.

What happens if you dial 666?
You will get some policemen upside down.

Teacher: Give me a sentence with 'judicious'.
*Matthew: Hands that judicious can be soft as your
face.*

What did King Henry do when he came to the throne?
He sat on it.

What did the beaver say to the tree?
It's been nice gnawing you.

What pop group kills household germs?
The Bleach Boys.

During dinner at the Ritz,
Father kept on having fits.
And what made my sorrow greater,
I was left to tip the waiter.

Where should a dressmaker build her house?
On the outskirts of the city.

What does the word 'minimum' mean?
A very small mother.

Waiter, waiter, why can't we have some light
   music while we eat?
*Certainly, madam. I'll go and plug the musicians into
   the lamp-socket.*

Can you find six well-known football teams here?

Cheasternm duneit, Veilporol, Esnalar, Teenvor, Hingmatton Setorf, Matnetoth Stophur.

What do you get if you cross a skeleton and a
    famous detective?
Sherlock Bones.

I know everything about football.
Okay, how many holes are there in a goal net?

Batty Books

The Roman Kidnapper by Caesar Quick
The Loud Bang by Dina Mite
Training a Parrot by L. O. Polly
My Pants Fell Down by Lucy Lastic
Bubbles in the Bath by Ivor Windy Bottom
Late Home by Mr Bus
Will He Win? by Betty Wont

Doctor: You must take four teaspoonfuls of this
   medicine before every meal.
Patient: But we've only got three teaspoons.

What's awarded to designers of door knockers?
The no-bell prize.

What do you call a man who wears a coat?
Mac.

What do you call a man who wears two coats?
Max.

Why did the apple turn over?
Because he saw the jam roll.

What do Red Indians put on themselves after
  they have had a bath?
Scalpum powder.

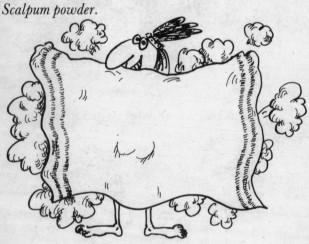

Doctor, doctor, I want to play snooker.
Then go to the end of the queue.

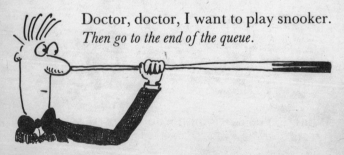

What is the animal with the highest
   intelligence?
A giraffe.

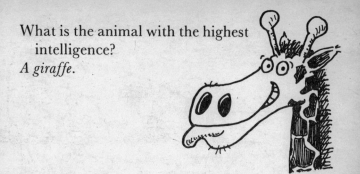

There is a donkey at the end of a cliff. There is a
   500-foot drop and at the bottom there is no
   ladder and the two cliffs are too far apart to
   jump. How did the donkey get across?
. . . You give up? . . . So did the donkey.

What did the doctor prescribe to the sick pig?
Oinkment!

Mum: How was your first day of school?
*Johnny: It was all right, except for a bloke called Sir
who kept spoiling the fun.*

Which way is it to the Professor's machine?

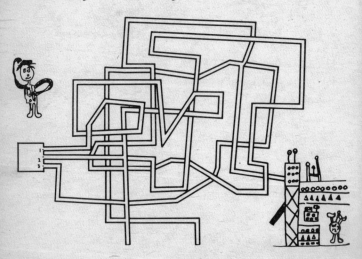

Don't eat school dinners,
Just throw them aside.
A lot of kids didn't,
A lot of kids died.
The meat's made of iron,
The spuds made of steel,
And if they don't kill you,
The puddings will!

'What are you doing with that manure?' said
the boy to the gardener.
'I'm putting it on my rhubarb,' replied the gardener.
'Really?' said the boy. 'Where I live we put
custard on it.'

What do you get if you pour hot water down a
rabbit hole?
Hot-cross bunnies.

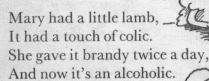

What is out of bounds?
An exhausted kangaroo.

Mary had a little lamb,
It had a touch of colic.
She gave it brandy twice a day,
And now it's an alcoholic.

Why didn't a man swim on an empty stomach?
Because it is easier to swim in water.

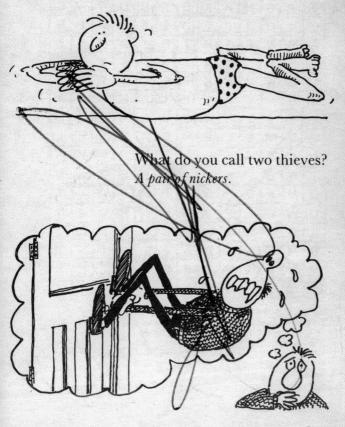

What do you call two thieves?
A pair of nickers.

A man goes to the doctor and says, 'I always
 have this dream about a door with a sign on
 it. I keep on pulling and pulling the door, but
 for some reason I cannot open it.'
'What does the sign say?' asked the doctor.
'Push.'

Word Search on Animals

F	P	S	N	A	K	E	F	R	G	O	M	C
C	A	O	S	P	P	O	E	E	O	B	P	H
C	B	N	R	T	H	T	R	I	R	H	R	E
A	E	E	D	T	A	T	R	N	I	Y	E	E
M	S	K	U	N	K	E	E	D	L	E	R	T
E	U	V	Z	L	E	R	T	E	L	S	T	A
L	T	I	G	E	R	E	Z	E	A	E	F	H
M	D	M	L	L	E	N	C	R	C	L	L	F
L	L	E	A	Z	F	L	E	V	O	O	V	A
T	T	B	E	N	M	T	E	S	U	Z	W	S
Q	U	F	S	R	O	N	P	P	S	W	A	N
U	W	O	L	F	U	W	S	H	H	C	Z	N
S	D	Q	S	T	O	R	K	E	Z	A	W	L
P	H	Q	A	W	R	A	T	Y	A	I	N	M
M	H	P	G	V	C	R	P	H	M	L	L	H	T
E	M	U	J	W	K	L	L	A	X	N	T	O

Can you find the following words:

cheetah	reindeer	deer	tiger	stork
emu	dog	ferret	cow	swan
elephant	seal	rat	otter	wolf
snake	skunk	gorilla	camel	

Doctor, doctor, my tongue feels like a pack of
   cards.
Go to the window and stick it out.
Will that help?
No, I just hate the man opposite.

What did the boy octopus say to the girl
   octopus?
I wanna hold your hand, hand, hand, hand, hand,
   hand, hand, hand.

Doctor, doctor, I only have fifty-nine seconds to
   live.
Wait a minute, I'll get the pills.

Name a famous French ant.
Napoleant.

What's green and brown and if it fell out of a
   tree on your head it would kill you?
A snooker table.

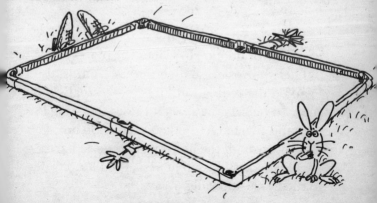

A man just released from prison was so elated after five years behind bars that he ran down the street shouting, 'I'm free! I'm free!' And then a small boy on the corner said, 'So what. I'm four!'

What is long and green and goes hith-hith?
A snake with a lisp.

There is a town with a house in it which has no windows or doors. How does the man get out? He jumps up so high that he bumps his head on the ceiling until it is really, really sore. So he gets the saw and saws the table in half and two halves make a whole. So he climbs through the hole and shouts so hard that he makes himself hoarse, then he gets on to the horse and rides away.

What do you call a boomerang that doesn't come back?
A stick!

Why did the bull rush?
Because it saw the cow slip!

Tongue Twister

Beth believes thieves seize skis.

Boy: Grandma, what's a weapon?
Grandma: A weapon is something you fight with.
Boy: You mean like Grandad?

What do you call a monkey with bananas in his
ears?
Anything you want because he can't hear you.

What do ghosts eat in an Italian restaurant?
Spook-ghetti!

Teacher: Kevin, why are you late for school?

Kevin: Well, sir, I was dreaming about this football match and I went into extra-time so I had to see the finish!

What did the burglar say when he was caught stealing the cutlery?

'I am at your service, madam.'

There was a young girl called Amba,
Who charmed a snake – a mamba.
With a hypnotic glance,
She made the snake dance,
To a rumba, tango and samba.

Why did the hedgehog cross the road?
To show it had guts.

Word Search

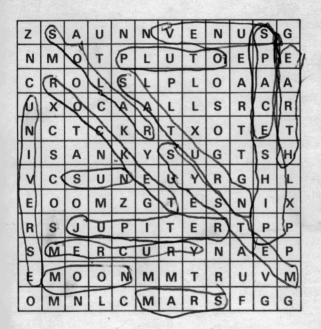

Z	S	A	U	N	N	V	E	N	U	S	G
N	M	O	T	P	L	U	T	O	E	P	E
C	R	O	L	S	L	P	L	O	A	A	A
U	X	O	C	A	A	L	L	S	R	C	R
N	C	T	C	K	R	T	X	O	T	E	T
I	S	A	N	K	Y	S	U	G	T	S	H
V	C	S	U	N	E	U	Y	R	G	H	L
E	O	O	M	Z	G	T	E	S	N	I	X
R	S	J	U	P	I	T	E	R	T	P	P
S	M	E	R	C	U	R	Y	N	A	E	P
E	M	O	O	N	M	M	T	R	U	V	M
O	M	N	L	C	M	A	R	S	F	G	G

Can you find the following words:

rocket   Mars   Sun
spaceship   Jupiter   Moon
Venus   Saturn   solar system
Mercury   Pluto   universe
space   Earth

27

Teacher: Tom, if you mowed seventeen
    people's lawns and they each gave you £1.50
    what would you get?
Tom: A new bike!

Knock, knock.
Who's there?
Doctor.
Doctor Who?
Ah, you know my name!

There was a young man from Bengal,
Who was invited to a fancy-dress ball.
He dressed up as a bun,
And went to the fun,
But a dog ate him up in the hall.

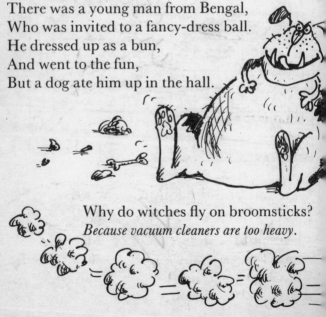

Why do witches fly on broomsticks?
Because vacuum cleaners are too heavy.

Doctor, doctor, I keep thinking I'm a parrot.
Just perch yourself there – I'll tweet you in a minute!

That girl over there just rolled her eyes at me.
Well, roll them back, she might need them.

What is the easiest way to count a large herd of cattle?
Use a cowculator.

What is the equator?
An imaginary lion running round the earth.

If a prehistoric monster took an exam, he'd
  pass with extinction.

What did the policeman say to his stomach?
You're under a vest!

Doctor, doctor, my dog swallowed a large bottle of aspirins. What should I do?
Try to give him a big headache.

What's big, hairy and can fly?
King Kongcorde.

What do bees demand?
More honey and less working flowers.

31

Where do sheep get their hair cut?
The baa baas.

How does an airline pilot's child finish his
　　prayers?
*God bless Mummy, God bless Daddy, God bless me,
　　over and out.*

Why did the football manager flood the pitch?
So he could bring on the sub!

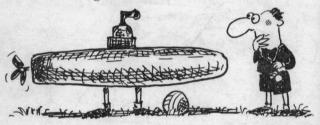

Mother Monster to Baby Monster: Do not eat
　　your chicken with your fingers, eat the
　　fingers separately.

An Englishman was on holiday in Scotland. His car broke down in a remote part of the Highlands. He could not find the problem with the engine, so he sat down by the side of the road and waited for someone to pass. Two hours later a Scottish shepherd passed by. 'Excuse me, are you a mechanic?' he asked the shepherd. 'Och, mun, dinnae be daft! I'm nae a Macanic, I'm a MacDougal!'

What flies and wobbles?
A Jellycopter.

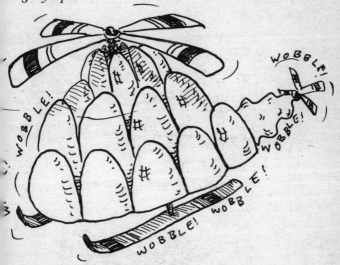

What do you do with a blue banana?
Try and cheer it up!

Knock, knock.
Who's there?
Keith.
Keith who?
Keith me, thweetheart.

There was a young man called Joel,
Who once went to the North Pole.
He was eaten by a polar bear,
And lost all his hair,
And that was the end of poor Joel!

Why can't you fool a snake?
Because it hasn't got any legs to pull.

What did the baby porcupine say when he
backed into a cactus?
Is that you, Mum?

What did one strawberry say to the other
  strawberry?
If it wasn't for you, I wouldn't be in this jam.

Teacher: There was the Ice Age, the Stone Age
  and what was next?
George: The sausage.

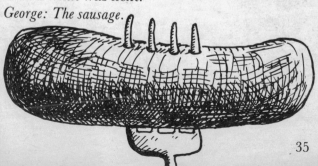

How do you fit four elephants
into a car?
Two in the front and two in the back!

Who ate his victims two by two?
Noah Shark.

What is a polygon?
A dead parrot.

What do you call a row of men waiting for a
haircut?
A barbercue.

How does a monster begin?
With an 'm'.

Knock, knock.
Who's there?
Yodley.
Yodley who?
I didn't know you could yodel.

What's grey and has a trunk?
A mouse going on holiday.

There was a young man from the west,
With hair like a mat on his chest.
It pricked like a pin,
And scratched his skin,
But at least he never needed a vest.

Mrs Wright: I would like a pair of alligator shoes.
Shop Assistant: Certainly, madam. What size does your alligator wear?

Who invented gun powder?
A lady who wanted guns to look pretty.

Where do ships go when they are ill?
To the 'docks'.

What did one tooth say to the other?
The dentist is taking me out tonight!

Knock, knock.
Who's there?
Luke.
Luke who?
Luke through the key-hole and you will find
   out!

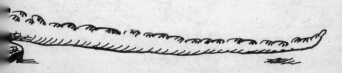

What do punks learn at school?
Punctuation.

Doctor, doctor, I feel like a bridge.
What's come over you?
Two lorries, one motorbike and a scooter!

If a king sits on gold, then who sits on silver?
The Lone Ranger.

What does an elephant do when he gets stuck
   up a tree?
He waits till autumn and then floats down on a leaf.

What did the cookie say to the biscuit?
Oh crumbs.

Why can't you ever go out with a salad?
Because it's always dressing.

A man dashed into a café and asked for a glass of water. He ran out without drinking it and came in for another. When the lady serving behind the counter asked him to drink it inside, he replied: 'It's not to drink, my house is on fire.'

There were two bishops in a bed. Which one wore the nightie?
Mrs Bishop.

When you're dancing,
With your honey,
And his nose,
Is rather runny,
Don't think it's very funny,
Because it's snot.

Do you say the yolk of an egg is white, or the yolk of an egg are white?
(Think about it.)

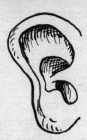 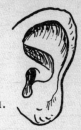

Knock, knock.
Who's there?
Ears.
Ears who?
Ears looking at you.

What happens if you walk under a cow?
I don't know, what happens if you walk under a cow?
You get a pat on the head.

What do you call a Chinese chip?
A stir fri.

Why did the angel lose his job?
Because of harp failure.

43

Knock, knock.
Who's there?
Thumb.
Thumb who?
Thumb like it hot, thumb like it cold . . .

How do you sink a stupid submarine?
Knock on the door.

Where do teenagers go for their holidays?
I don't know, where do teenagers go for their holidays?
Acney.

44

A duck goes to a library every day, taking back
    one book and taking out another. After a
    while, the librarian gets suspicious and
    follows the duck. They come to a large frog
    on a lily leaf with a pile of books saying:
    'Read it! Read it!'

Two men were walking in the street. One says,
    'I know a man with a wooden leg named
    Smith,' and the other man says, 'Really,
    what's the name of his other leg?'

Mrs Wright: Timmy, did you take a bath
    today?
Timmy: Why, is one missing?

There was once a schoolboy called Kidd,
Who ate twenty pies for a quid.
When they asked, are you faint,
He replied, no I ain't,
But I don't feel as well as I did.

Why do bees hum?
Because they have forgotten the words.

Why do bees have sticky hair?
Because of the honey comb!

What goes zubb zubb?
A bee flying backwards.

ZUBB ZUBB!

There was a family, Mr Bigger, Mrs Bigger and
    Baby Bigger.
Which was bigger?
Baby Bigger – he was a little bigger.

Why did the chicken cross the road?
To get to the other side.

Why did the shark cross the road?
Because he was tied to the chicken.

What did the duck say when she bought some lipstick?
Put it on the bill.

How do you get a baby astronaut to sleep?
Rock it.

A cat must have three tails. You don't believe me? Listen: any cat has more tails than no cat, right? And no cat has two tails, right? So any cat must have three tails.

Puzzle

1. Something you go abroad on.
2. Something you ride.
3. It gives you milk.
4. It keeps you warm.
5. You get bacon from it.
6. You get wool from it.
7. It's called the King of the Jungle.
8. It's man's best friend.
9. It eats chickens.

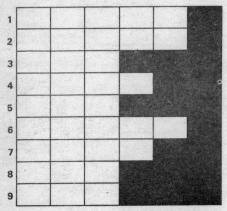

My budgie lays square eggs.
That's amazing! Can it talk as well?
Yes, but only one word.
What's that?
Ouch!

Mr Roberts: I'll pay you 20p to clean my car
this week, and next week I'll raise it to 30p.
John: Right, I'll start next week.

What happens to people who learn about
mummies?
They get all wrapped up in their work.

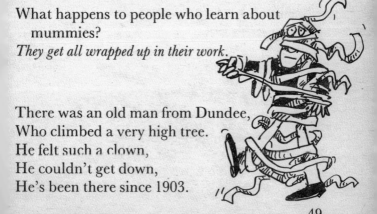

There was an old man from Dundee,
Who climbed a very high tree.
He felt such a clown,
He couldn't get down,
He's been there since 1903.

49

I was very ill in China.
What did you have?
Kung flu.

'James, do we get fur from skunks?' asked the
    teacher.
'Yes,' he replied. 'We get as fur away as we can.'

How do you know when the tide goes out?
It gives a little wave.

What do you get when your mum's buns have
    burnt in the oven?
A hot-cross mum.

What do you call a man with a number plate on
    his head?
Reg.

What does his mum call him?
R Reg.

What do you call a burning jacket?
A blazer.

Have you got any invisible ink?
Certainly, sir, what colour?

Where was Solomon's temple?
On the side of his head.

Mary: You remind me of the sea.
Fred: You mean I'm romantic?
Mary: No, you make me sick.

How did seven fat ladies fit under an umbrella
and not get wet?
When it wasn't raining.

What's furry and minty?
A Polo bear.

What is green and hairy and shouts, 'Help!
  Help!'
A gooseberry in a swimming pool.

Why is a baby like Maradona?
Because it's good at dribbling.

Why do you keep throwing bunches of garlic
  out the window?
To keep the vampires away.
But there are no vampires here.
Jolly effective, isn't it?

I won't say that our school dinners are bad, but even the bins have ulcers!

Aagh! Mum! I just got ELECTROCUTED!
How shocking.
Mum, you're revolting.
Watt?

What do you call a monster lying in a gutter?
Dwayne.

Word Search

c	r	a	b	b	i	t	o
f	h	o	a	l	i	o	n
h	d	o	t	r	m	m	d
o	e	c	s	i	p	l	c
r	e	h	o	q	g	n	b
s	r	o	r	x	z	e	a
e	f	o	t	q	r	s	r
s	o	d	o	g	p	q	f
m	n	s	r	t	o	u	h

Can you find the following words:

rabbit   dog   horse   deer
bat   tiger   lion

SWAG

Knock, knock.
Who's there?
Burglar.
Burglar who?
Burglar doesn't knock.

Why did the Egyptian girl cry?
Because her daddy was a mummy.

There was an old lady from Birkin,
Who was very fond of small gherkins.
One day at tea,
She ate forty-three,
And pickled her entire workins.

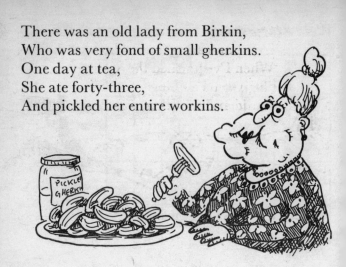

What time is it when you meet a crocodile?
Time to run!

Teacher: If we breath oxygen in the daytime,
    what do we breath at night?
Sam: Nitrogen.

Why did the chicken cross the road?
To practise his running!

'Open wide,' said a dentist called Bert,
To a man-eating shark whose teeth hurt,
'When I've finished the drilling,
I'll give you a filling.'
He did and the filling was Bert.

What flies across the washing-line at 200 miles
  per hour?
Honda pants!

A humourless teacher called Mills,
Cured insomnia without using pills.
His words dull and boring,
Led quickly to snoring,
For such were his medical skills.

What do you call a man who inspects eggs?
An Eggspector!

What vegetable do you peel, then cook, then
eat, then throw away?
Corn on the cob.

What did the farmer call his two rows of
cabbages?
A dual cabbageway.

Have you heard the joke about the pencil?
There's no point in telling you!

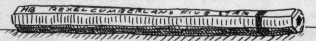

Crossword Puzzle

ACROSS

1. Which bird lays the biggest eggs?
4. What noise do sheep make?
5. What is the opposite of lose?
6. What is the fastest bird?
7. French for eleven.
8. Another name for God.
9. The god of the sea.

DOWN

1. Which bird is said to be wise?
2. What vehicles were used before buses?
3. From what animal do we get steak?
4. What did Richard Branson fly across the Atlantic in?
10. Where do shopkeepers put their money?
11. What do you fasten trousers with?
12. The first number.
13. A female deer.
14. A sticky black substance used for making roads.

ANSWERS
ACROSS 1. ostrich 4. bleat 5. win 6. swift 7. onze 8. Lord 9. Neptune
DOWN 1. owl 2. trams 3. cow 4. balloon 10. till 11. zip 12. one 13. doe 14. tar

What do you say when you meet a two-headed monster?
Hello, hello.

When is it dangerous to go into your garden?
When the buds are shooting.

What comes after a sea-horse?
A dee-horse.

Why did the chicken cross the road?
To get the Chinese newspaper.
Do you get it?
Neither do I.
We get *The Times.*

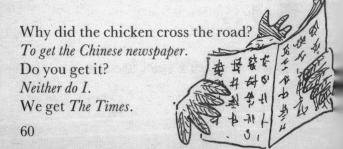

What happened when the lady washed her
    doorstep?
She broke the washing-machine.

What has seven trunks, twenty-eight feet and
    fourteen ears?
A herd of elephants.

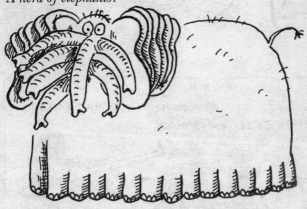

What did the Spanish farmer say to his hen?
Olé.

What jewels do ghosts wear?
Tombstones.

Teacher: Who was Turner's Close named
    after?
Boy: Tina Turner, sir.

There was an old man of Blackheath,
Who sat on his set of false teeth,
Said he with a start,
'O Lord bless my heart,
I have bitten myself underneath.'

Why did the banana cross the road?
Because he was being chased by an elephant!

What goes 150 miles per hour under water?
A motorpike.

Knock, knock.
Who's there?
Dishwasher.
Dishwasher who?
Dishwasher the way I spoke before I had my
braces.

Why do bees buzz?
Because they can't hum.

Why did the boy want turkey?
Because he was feeling a bit peckish.

Word Search

```
t c a p e z e t r a n t p a c
r i n g m a s t e r z e p w l
k r g t t a p z e e e z u p o
o c k h i t w u o w o t p a w
s u t t h e a n m m a l s n
k s s u b r t i o n k o w s s
t o k b i g o t u p o s o k e
k o b i g t o p w s p o w k e
r z u w l e z e e t v p e z i
e l k u a k o v e l u p k o w
z p u k o z e k t r a p e z e
a e o k a n i m a l z i m a l
o z s p a p n p i p m p a p l
e e p s o w k e p l o w k s b
l i o n w k o e l e p h a n t
```

Can you find the following words:

tightrope	clowns	trapeze
lion	circus	animal
ringmaster	big top	elephant

Tongue Twister

Tall Tommy Tortoise talked to Timmy Turtle
on the telephone ten times today.

Why did the monkey fall out of the tree?
Because he was dead!

Why did the chicken fall out of the tree?
Because he was stapled to the monkey!

Why did the elephant fall out of the tree?
Because he thought it was a game!

Why is the longest nose only eleven inches?
Otherwise it would be a foot!

A flea and a fly in a flue
Were trapped, so they thought, 'What to do?'
'Let us fly,' said the flea.
'Let us flee,' said the fly.
So they flew through a flaw in the flue.

Hickory dickory dock,
Three mice ran up the clock.
The clock struck one
And the other two got away with minor
    injuries.

There was a young fellow named Max,
Who filled up his pockets with tacks.
He thought he was clever,
Although he could never,
Sit down in his chair and relax.

Knock, knock.
Who's there?
Arthur.
Arthur who?
Arthur gotten!

What do cannibals play?
Swallow my leader.

First Vampire: A beggar came up to me and
   claimed he hadn't had a bite in days.
Second Vampire: What did you do?
First Vampire: What could I do? I bit him.

Doctor, doctor, my son has just swallowed a
  ballpoint pen.
I'll be right over.
What shall I do until you arrive?
Use a pencil!

Batty Books

When Shall We Meet Again by Miles Apart
The Arctic Ocean by I. C. Waters
The Haunted Room by Hugo First
Knocked Out by Esau Stars

Dead Funny

Did you hear about:
The tobacconist who snuffed it,
The cleaner who bit the dust,
The frogman who croaked,
The footballer who passed on,
The abseiler who came to the end of his rope,
The window-cleaner who kicked the bucket.

Last night someone drilled a hole in the fence
    surrounding a nudist camp.
The police are looking into it.

Why was Cinderella no good at football?
Because her coach was a pumpkin.

What fish helps musicians?
A tuna fish.

A Welshman known as Dai
Threw a custard pie
At Uncle Jack
Who threw it back
Right into Dai's right eye.

So, you say you do the best
'Disappearing Act'....

How many punk-rockers does it take to screw
  in a lightbulb?
*Two: one to screw in the lightbulb and one to kick the
  chair away.*

Why did the chicken cross the road?
It wanted to lose weight.

There were three men who wanted to marry the same woman. The first said, 'Can I marry you?' The woman said, 'Only if you jump off the cliff,' so he jumped off the cliff. The second man did the same thing. The third man asked her the same thing as the first man and the second man, and the woman said, 'Only if you jump off the cliff.' The third man said, 'Ladies first.'

A famous painter met his death,
Because he couldn't draw his breath.

Mark: If I lay one egg on this chair and two on the table, how many will I have altogether?
Felix: Personally, I don't believe you can do it.

There was an old lady from Fife,
Who had never been kissed in her life.
Along came a cat,
And she said, 'I'll kiss that!'
But the cat answered, 'Not on your life!'

Teacher: If I gave you three rabbits and then
the next day I gave you five rabbits, how
many would you have?
Girl: Nine, miss.
Teacher: Nine?
Girl: Yes, miss. I've already got one.

Have you heard the story about the brick wall?
I'd better not tell you, you will never get over it.

Knock, knock.
Who's there?
Dishes.
Dishes who?
Dishes my last joke!

She stood by the bridge at midnight,
Her lips were all a-quiver.
She gave a cough,
Her leg fell off,
And floated down the river.

Where does a general keep his armies?
Up his sleevies.

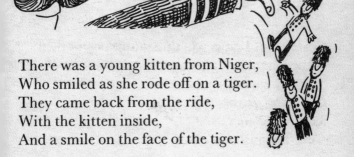

There was a young kitten from Niger,
Who smiled as she rode off on a tiger.
They came back from the ride,
With the kitten inside,
And a smile on the face of the tiger.

Do you know the joke about butter? Shall I tell
you?
I am not going to tell it to you because you'll spread it.

Knock, knock.
Who's there?
Oscar.
Oscar who?
Oscar silly question you get a silly answer.

Why did the elephant cross the road?
Because he wanted to sit on the chicken.

Daft Definitions

Air: a balloon with its skin off.
A Jet-setter: a flying dog.
Cabaret: a row of taxis.
Discover: a cover for a record.
Halfwit: someone who's funny half the time.

Why did the Indian put a bucket over his head?
He wanted to be a paleface.

Where were potatoes first found?
In the ground.

There was an old man from Bath,
Who had the funniest laugh.
While eating his dinner,
He found he got thinner,
Until he was only half.

What did the man say to the bottle and why
  was he cross?
I don't know, what did the man say to the bottle and
  why was he cross?
I'm drunk because of you.

How do you catch a squirrel?
Kneel on the floor and make a noise like an acorn.

THE FIRST UNDER WATER SPY!

I know what I'll do... I'll be an under water spy

GLUB, GLUB, GLUB!

Calling 007!
JAMES POND to the rescue!

Mary had a kitten,
Tommy had a pup,
Alphonse had a crocodile,
Which ate the others up.

MEOW!!

What's a crocodile's favourite game?
Snap.

Why did the cucumber blush?
'Cos it saw the salad dressing.

Why was the burglar so alarmed?
Because he heard the burglar alarm.

What kind of medicine does Dracula take for
   coughs?
Coffin medicine.

What do you give a sick bird?
Tweetment.

Why does a stork stand on one foot?
Because if he lifted the other foot, he'd fall down.

What do policemen like in their sandwiches?
Truncheon meat.

Doctor: I'm afraid you've got only three
    minutes to live.
Man: Is there nothing you can do for me?
Doctor: I could boil you an egg.

What did the big telephone say to the little
    telephone?
You're too young to be engaged!

Why did the farmer drive his steam-roller over his field?
He wanted to grow mashed potatoes.

BURRP!

What's a frog's favourite drink?
Croak-a-cola.

How do you fall off a fifty-foot ladder without hurting yourself?
Fall off the bottom step.

How do we know that Prince Charles was a cry-baby when he was young?
Because he's the Prince of Wales.

WAAA!

What is the name of the football team who have never met each other before the match?
Queen's Park Strangers.

Why did the vicar walk on his hands?
It was Palm Sunday.

What can never be made right?
Your left ear.

Roses are red,
Violets are blue,
I can row a boat, canoe?

What animal needs oiling?
Mice, because they squeak.

Knock, knock.
Who's there?
Pooh.
Pooh who?
Don't cry, these jokes are almost over.

There was a bald kitten called Neil,
Who went for a ride on a seal.
He would have survived,
If the seal hadn't dived,
And the shark hadn't wanted a meal!

The art of gentle persuasion...

A Cowboy's Adventure

An intrepid cowboy was riding through Deadman's Gulch, when he was attacked by a marauding band of Sioux Indians. With the odds at 5,000 to 1, he found that he was slightly outnumbered. He fought bravely, but eventually he was beaten to the ground and captured.

Chief Sitting Bull was most impressed with the cowboy's courage and promised him the honour of a slow, painful death.

The cowboy's clothes were ripped from his body and he was buried up to his neck in the coarse desert sand. For two days the sun blistered his face and caused his thirsty tongue to swell; for two nights the freezing wind chilled his very marrow.

At last the Indian chief returned, ready to exhume the body. He was surprised to find the cowboy very much alive and in control of his faculties. He was hauled out of the hole and accorded much honour.

'I shall grant you one pleasure,' said Sitting Bull. 'Perhaps a dropeen of 33-year-old firewater? Or a dance with my voluptuous daughter, Howling Wolf?'

The cowboy desired no more than a few words in the ear of his trusty steed.

His horse was brought to him. He whispered

into the stallion's ear, and the fine animal raced away across the desert sand.

'Don't worry,' said our hero. 'Muffin will return within two hours with something that will surprise you all.'

Sure enough, faithful Muffin returned . . . bearing a black kitten on his back.

Quick thinking was needed!

'A gift for you, wise Chief – to keep the mice from nibbling at your wigwam!'

Sitting Bull looked at the cowboy in admiration. That anyone could be so generous, in the face of death! He therefore was magnanimous and granted the cowboy his freedom.

As the cowboy rode off into the sunset, he bent over the horse's neck and shouted into his ear: 'Muffin, you're a real dope – I said get a "posse", not a "pussy"!'

What's the definition of benign?
It's what you can't wait to be when you're eight!

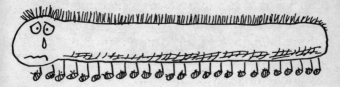

What's worse than a giraffe with a sore throat?
A centipede with chilblains!

What do you get if you cross a cocker spaniel, a
poodle and a rooster?
Cockerpoodledo . . .

What's the best thing to give as a parting gift?
A comb.

There was a fine guinea pig named Yoffi,
Who was frightfully partial to toffee.
The kids said, 'How clever,
His teeth stick together,
Let's try him on cognac and coffee.'

Why has a polar bear got a fur coat?
'Cos he'd look silly in a plastic mac!

Two buckets of sick on a bus.
Bucket One: Why are you crying?
Bucket Two: I get really sad when I come round this way.
Bucket One: Why's that?
Bucket Two: Well, I was brought up around here!

What's green, hairy and goes up and down?
A gooseberry in a lift!

What sits in a fruit bowl and shouts for help?
A damson in distress.

Waiter, how long will my sausages be?
I don't know, sir, I never measure them.

Why did the foal cough?
Because he was a little hoarse.

What is yellow and stupid?
Thick custard.

The devils challenged the angels to a cricket match. 'Don't be silly,' said an angel, 'surely you realize that we have all the best cricketers up here?' 'Ah, yes!' replied one of the devils, 'but guess where all the best umpires are?'

What do you call a man with a paper-bag on
    his head?
Russell.

What do you call a man with a seagull on his
    head?
Cliff!

Old Age – When One is Eight

'Mr B., were you in the war?'
'Yes.'
'Did Queen Victoria give you a medal?'

Cheek – and Stuff

'Mr B., when I told my dad you said you were no good at playing rugby, he wasn't surprised – he just said, "As well?"'

'When did you come to this school, Mr B.?'
'William of Normandy brought me over.'
'That's William the Conqueror, isn't it?'
'Yes.'
'I never liked *him*.'

'Hey, Mr B., you know when you tell us to eat our lunch and we'll get good-looking like you?'
'Yes.'
'Shall I tell you why we eat it?'
'Oh, all right.'
'It's because we know it won't come true. You get, Mr B.?'

Patient: I'm suffering from loss of memory.
Doctor: How long has this been going on?
Patient: How long has *what* been going on?

What do hedgehogs eat for lunch?
Prickled onions!

How do you make a band stand?
Take their chairs away.

What animal drops from the clouds?
Raindeer.

What has four legs and cannot walk?
A chair.

What did you get on your birthday?
A year older . . .

Teacher: Give me a sentence with the word
'gruesome' in it.
Charlie: The man stopped shaving and gruesome
whiskers.

A Corny Story

A cruel young chap from Heathrow,
Had a corn on the side of his toe;
When he had it cut out,
It replied (with a shout),
'You could have just *asked* me to go!'

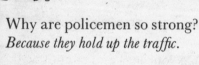
Where do birds invest their money?
In the stork market!

Why are policemen so strong?
Because they hold up the traffic.

Why is a boxer like a candle?
Because one blow – and he's out!

Teacher: Johnny, I wish you'd pay a little
attention.
Johnny: I'm paying as little attention as I can, miss.

Gary, did your sister help you with your
   homework?
No, miss, she did it all!

Why can a leopard never get out of a zoo?
Because it's always spotted!

What is hail?
Hard boiled rain.

What are hippies for?
To keep your leggies up!

Where do policemen live?
999 Letsby Avenue!

Teacher: If you have 40p in one pocket and 50p in the other, what would you have?

Boy: *Someone else's trousers, sir!*

Mrs Wright: Can I put this wallpaper on myself?

Assistant: *Yes, madam, but it would look a lot better on the wall!*

Our thanks to Tim Patton, Tim Lewis, Dave Baldwin and all of the teachers, staff and children of St Anthony's School, Hampstead, who made this book possible.

A.L. and R.M.

List of Contributors

The Children

Benji Aird-Fairley
Marcus Allander
Gaby Altschuler
Adam Arnold
Michael As'ad

Oliver Bailey
Max Baird-Smith
John Balmond
Mark Barber
Daniel Bardiger
Nii Barnor
Paul Barry
Dominic Bastyra
Dominik Bauch
Tommy Benz
Paul Beresford
Daniel Berzon
Jo Betteridge
Mehul Bhimjiyani
James Bland
Ali Boroumand
William Borrell
Ben Brafman
Julian Brewster

James Castles
Wayne Cheng
Ben Chik
Alex Chinn
Irial Chung
Jon Clogg
James Cooper
Dominic Corley
Alex Costa
Barnie Cowling

Andrew Cox
Hugh Cox
Matthew Craven-Walker
Ben Cussins
Timothy Cussins

Amir Daftari
Peter Damouni
Dominic Dandridge
Kooros Daneshva
Eddie Davis
Oliver Dewhurst
Shiva Dindyal
Tariq Dudhia

Simon Eder
Nick Edwards
Nicky Eliades
Hugo Elias
Georg Ell
Andrew Emery
Jamie Ettedgui

James Fishberg
Paul Fishman
Timmy Frank
Daniel Freedman
Andrew Freiberger
Ben Frommer-Dawson
Ciaran Frost
Liam Frost
Pascal Furness

Simon Galan
Olivier Galbinski
Oscar Galbinski

Dave Garcia
James Gilbert
Adam Gishen
Toby Glyn
Jon Goldsmith
David Goodliffe
Tom Gore
Daniel Grant
Sam Gray
Jake Green
James Grey

Kit Hanson
Adam Harris
Oliver Harris
Benjamin Hart
Kit Hawkins
Akio Hayakawa
Corin Hehel
Luke Hersheson
Alex Hooper-Hodson
Michael Hopkins

Ben Immanuel

Jesse Jacobson
Scott Jacobson
Jonny Jenkins
Leo Johnson

Andrew Kanaber
Daniel Kanaber
Oliver Karger
Benji Katz
Joshua Katz
Robbie Katz
Elliot Kaye
Timmy Kellow
Robert Kelly
Adam Kershaw

Jason Lai
Dominic Lake la Hausse

Jamie Lawson

Adam Leadercramer
Alex Leech
Simon Leech
James Legge
Sam Leifer
Dimitris Lemos
Jamie Lewis
Toby Lichtig
David Lissauer
Daniel Livitsky
Matthew Lowe
Max Lucas

Edward McCann
Timmy Malachard
Freddy Mandy
Will Mandy
Aldo Mansi
James Manton
Marco Maranzana
Hugh Mark
Jeff Mark
Joshua Martin
Anthony Maxwell
Nicholas Michael
Andrew Mindel
Michael Miranda
Joel Mishcon
Chris Mitchell
Matthew James Mizzi
Simon Mizzi
Nima Mokhtarzadeh
Benji Morris
Luke Mortner
Charlie Myers

Timothy Nedas
Jonathan Newman
Arize Nwandu

Conor O'Connor

Niall O'Connor
Luke Osborne

Henry Paker
Simon Palmiero
Nicholas Pawlik
Adrian Peskin
Damian Petsas
Christos Phillipou
Jeremy Phillips
Joseph Phillips
Matthew Phillips
Finn Pollard
Max Porter

Iman Rahmani
Orang Rahmani
Joe Randall-Cutler
Asher Raybould
Joshua Raymond
Andrew Redman
Theo Ricketts
Chris Robinson
Kieren Robinson
Adam Rochford
Justin Rose
Toby Rose
Adam Rosenthal
Danny Rottman

Benedict Samuel
Joshua Samuel
Ben Shipton
Oliver Shipton
Adam Shipway

Mark Shulman
Gabriel Silver
Rupinder Singh Vig
Jesse Singleton
Marc Souter
Peter Steele Lopez
Anthony Stiefel
Gary Stiefel
Simon Peter Stobart
Erick Stossel
Joe Sumner
Eiji Suzuki

Rafeek Tadios
Jeffrey Tannenbaum
Tom Tapply
Nima Tehranchi
Darius Thompson
Madoc Threipland
Graham Tilden
Charlie Tilley
Yosuke Togo

Toby Vansani

Oliver Walsh
Sam Weisfeld
James Welch
Oliver Winton
Francis Worth

Jamie Yap

Alan Zilouf
Andrew Zilouf

Teachers and Staff

Roger Allingham
Dell Attwood-Bloomfield
Dave Baldwin
Dominic Bell
Mr Bellamy
Sue Celaire
Judith Cohen
Leviu Galbinski
Maria Greensmith

Sheila Johnson
Leo Landman
Tim Lewis
Margaret McCann
Mary O'Brien
Clare Partington
Tim Patton
Helen Pitel
Nigel Pitel